Byrd Thou Never Wert

EMMETT BYRD

Byrd Thou Never Wert

The Collected Poems and Post Cards of Emmett Byrd

Compiled by Michael Hinden
Edited by John Crowe Byrd
and Winslow Farquhar

Ten Speed Press

Ten Speed Press
P.O. Box 7123
Berkeley, California 94707

Library of Congress Catalog Number 80-65365
ISBN 0-89815-023-X

Designed by Hal Hershey and Brenton Beck
Cover illustration by Pedro J. Gonzalez
Fifth Street Design Associates

ACKNOWLEDGMENTS

Several of Emmett's poems appeared originally in *Pucred*. Grateful acknowledgment is made to Dick Jesson, former "other editor," for his foresight, hindsight, and permission to reprint them. Grateful acknowledgment is also made to the Hawaiian who sings in the night.

M.C.H.

SECOND DEDICATION

And to the memory of Winslow Farquhar

J. C. B.

First Preface

When Winslow Farquhar enlisted my help in editing a critical edition of the poems of Emmett Byrd, he sensed from the start that he might never live to complete the project. Sadly, while this manuscript was still in the early stages of preparation, Winslow was eaten by a lion at the zoo. Like the poet he so admired, he was a young man of immense courage and considerable personal charm. In addition to this text, he left behind a wife, a child by a previous marriage, and two chapters of an unfinished dissertation.

Thus it fell upon my shoulders to complete the project begun by my collaborator. I take full responsibility for any and all errors in the text (except those in the Chronological Table and the Index of Titles and First Lines, which Winslow handled).

The poetry selections are arranged by chronological order in four groupings according to a plan agreed upon by Emmett Byrd and Farquhar. The notes accompanying the poems are located separately at the end of each section. They are addressed to the scholar as well as the general reader, and it is hoped they will prove useful to all.

I am indebted to Mrs. Emma Byrd, the poet's mother, for permission to publish selections from Emmett's correspondence. Her recent demise was yet another in a series of untimely losses.

J. C. B.

Second Preface

This long-awaited edition of the collected poems and post cards of Emmett Byrd was essentially complete and ready for the printer when my esteemed colleague, Professor John Crowe Byrd, swallowed a charcoal briquette at a barbeque in his honor and passed away unexpectedly.

My only contribution was to add the second preface, take care of postage, and correct proof.

Two fine scholars (one young and promising, the other old and having delivered) lost their lives during the preparation of this volume. In the act of publishing they gave their last full measure of devotion. We who are still in luck must carry on.

M. C. H.

Table of Contents

Introduction

The meager events of Emmett Byrd's life are recorded in the Chronological Table. He died by his own hand on his twenty-ninth birthday, but physical discomfort, prison, and a broken heart had darkened his poetic career long before that. He left behind only a handful of completed poems, but as critics have observed, the wonder was that he wrote any at all. At school he was a doodler and was taunted mercilessly by his fellow classmates for his clubfoot, lisp, and warts. He was last in his class to get hair under his arms. At fourteen he left school, and thereafter (until he entered Dakota University at the age of twenty-three) he seemed to hobble through life without an aim.

But then the poet in him blossomed, and within a year or two the tree bore fruit. About this time Emmett's post cards begin, and henceforth they are an indispensable accompaniment to his art. These post cards carry the ravages of wounds, passion, frustration, and despair. They are also marked by bad penmanship, though in most cases Farquhar and I have been able to decipher them.

At Dakota University Emmett joined, and was immediately cut from, the football team. Then he immersed himself in poetry. He read, and in turn was influenced by, Spenser, Shakespeare, Lovelace, and Marvell. He grew inordinately fond of the Romantics and could recite by heart long passages from Wordsworth, Coleridge, Shelley, Keats; though by all accounts, his voice had an unpleasant nasal twang. Among the Victorians he best liked Arnold, Tennyson, and Hopkins. Of the Moderns he admired Yeats, Eliot, Thomas, and Stevens. Echoes of all these poets can be found in Emmett's work. His real genius lies in the manner in which he was able to plunder his sources while giving form to his own poetic needs. In art as well as in life he took freely and without shame: indeed, that was his motto.

Although Emmett's early verse is not terribly original, it shows a degree of technical skill and ethical sensitivity rare in so youthful a writer. *Zapata and Enchilada,* the major achievement of this period, points toward the later maturation of his gifts.

For in the early spring of 1973 an amazing metamorphosis took place. In the space of a few months, out of the crucible of passion, despair, and sexual experiment, Emmett poured forth a lyrical display of astonishing vigor and complexity. His complete lack of poetical inhibitions, his clarity, force, and honest attention to naturalistic (even brutal) detail set these works apart from his earlier, more conventional verse. Properly speaking, these are love poems. And surely no poet since the nineteenth century has written so profoundly or explored with such a wealth of concrete images the subject of man's relationship to ducks.

It would be a mistake, however, to praise Emmett solely on the basis of his skill as a realistic chronicler of wild life. For Emmett nature is seen as emblematic, its physical features being symbols of a deep, mysterious moral and spiritual order. From his detailed observations of water fowl Emmett was able to derive sound moral precepts with universal appeal, as evidenced in his crowning achievement, the mature, somber, majestical *Ode To a Duck*. With this poem, written in the autumn of his final year, we can trace Emmett's growth from frustration and unhappiness, through passion and impetuosity, to the calm serenity of philosophical acceptance.

Of course, appearances can be deceiving. A few weeks later he was back in the dumps again and killed himself. But in no way does this sad event detract from the philosophic import of his poetry.

The process of Emmett's disintegration is recorded faithfully in his last work. Although some critics consider *Poem On His Twenty-Ninth Birthday* excessively gloomy, and certainly a step in the wrong direction, it nevertheless makes a fine epitath. It is the last (and perhaps most moving) document of the trials and tribulations of a very sensitive person.

J. C. B.

1944   October 31. Emmett born in a manger just outside Charleston, West Virginia. His father, Beauregard, a blacksmith, had in 1943 married Emma, daughter of John Ausfahrt, the stable owner. The bride wore an organdy dress and carried daisies.

1947   April 16. Father kicked in the head by a horse (dies).
April 17. Horse kicked in the head by Emmett (breaks his foot).
April 18. Horse shot.

1948   Emmett learns how to talk. His first words are: "Mama, Gimme a Pencil."

1956   Emmett expelled from school for writing bad words on the blackboard. An autodidact, he develops a passion for Browning.

1958   Emmett enrolled in Crowe Academy for Wayward Boys just outside Wheeling. An autodidact, he develops a passion for Arnold (his roommate). Expelled in February.

1959   March. Apprenticed to an apothecary, L. O. Kidd, in Charleston. Carries on friendship with C. C. Clopp, borrowing books and reading with him. Also borrows eighty dollars and carries on with Clopp's sister.

1960   Early attempts at verse. Translates the *Odyssey* (back into Greek).

1961   January. Slightly injured in a tavern brawl.

1962   Just hangs around.

1963   Visits Toronto with Clopp's sister. Grows a moustache.

1964   Gets clap. Breaks off with Clopp.

1965   Returns to Charleston.

1966   Develops a passion for garbanzo beans.

1967   Enrolls as a freshman at Dakota University on the advice of his uncle, John Crowe Byrd, professor.

1969   Develops a passion for his teaching assistant, Thelma Wapshingle. In May renounces the apothecary trade. In a letter to his mother writes: "I think I'll be a poet."

1970   June. Emmett graduates with honors (Valedictorian, Marching Band, Best Dressed Senior). He receives an electric razor from his mother and enrolls as a candidate for a Master of Fine Arts, completing his degree the following May.

1971   June. He is appointed Instructor of English at Dakota University, a post he retains until his death.

July-September. Emmett works on *Enchilada,* a romantic ballad.

October. Unable to finish *Enchilada,* Emmett gives the manuscript to Isidore Obermann, an assistant professor in the English Department.

November. Obermann loses the manuscript.

1972   February. *Lines Composed Upon an Early Morning Freshman English Class* published in *The Fulsome Messenger,* Fulsome, N.D.

March. Discovery of the *Enchilada* manuscript under a pile of underwear in Obermann's trunk.

April-December. Emmett revises *Enchilada*. The poem, now entitled *Zapata and Enchilada: A Romantic Ballad,* is completed on Christmas day.

December-January. Emmett spends Christmas vacation in Ft. Lauderdale.

1973   "The marvelous summer." From the spring to the autumn of 1973 Emmett, in a burst of brilliant creativity, completes a dozen poems, virtually the entire body of work for which he is remembered.

March 1. *Epithelmalamion* presented to Thelma as a birthday present. Emmett, Thelma, and Obermann celebrate until the wee hours of the morning.

April. Emmett, Thelma, and Obermann spend Easter in a cabin in the Dakota woods.

June 10. Thelma and Obermann elope to Nebraska. Emmett suffers a nervous breakdown. Develops a passion for ducks.

Late June. *Emmett and the Duck, Sonnet 1.*

July 4. Emmett vacations at Devil's Lake, N.D. There he writes *Rover Beach.*

Late July. *The Love Song of Emmett Byrd.* He develops hives.

Early August. *The Second Ducking.*

Mid August. *Ozzyduckias.* Emmett involved in another romantic entanglement.

Late August. *To His Coy Duck.*

Early September. *The Duckhover.*

September 10-24. Emmett spends two weeks

in jail on a variety of charges. Writes *To His Duck From Prison.*

Mid October. Emmett completes *Ode To a Duck.*

October 31. *Poem On His Twenty-Ninth Birthday.* Emmett plunges to his death. On his tombstone, by his command, these words are cut: "Emmett Byrd, M.F.A. 1944-1973. He took freely and without shame."

(W. F.)

Poems

BOOK ONE

Early Byrd

Zapata and Enchilada: A Romantic Ballad

The Argument

This poem, aiming to please,
has no argument with anyone.

Part I

In all of Spain was not, I wot, a
Lady sweet as Enchilada.
Ne'er was there a count who got a
Scent of fragrant Enchilada

A drunken sailor stopeth one in three and telleth thith tale.

Who did not upon the spot a-
Nnounce (without a taint or blot) a
Daring plan, some hopeless plot, a
Way to win sweet Enchilada.

It concerneth a lady.

So naturally when Count Zapata,
Captain of the Queen's Armada,
On the windy seas had got a
Pungent waft of Enchilada;

The Count geteth his first whiff.

So it was that this Zapata
Called out to his shipmate, Lotta:
"By the gods, I'm waxing hotter!
I must have this Enchilada!"

Then o'er the seas sailed Count Zapata
With his trusty shipmate Lotta
To the harbor of El Gada
And the cot of Enchilada.

The ship driven by a stiff wind (and crew) to the harbor of El Gada.

3

Part II.

There quoth Lotta to Zapata,
"O Zapata, wax not hot, sir!
Flee with me sir, to the sea, sir,
Give a thought to the regatta!"

*The salty Lotta
striveth to prevent
Zapata's folly.*

Alas, before the hot Zapata
Could e'er reply to salty Lotta,
At the threshold of the cot a-
Ppeared the lady Enchilada.

*But the Count
persisteth in
his madness.*

With haughty voice said Enchilada
To the gallant Count Zapata:
"Say to me who may it be, sir,
Reeking of the far salt sea, sir;

*And lo!
The lady appeareth
and speaketh to
the Count.*

"Say to me who quakes before me
Hot and ready to implore me
To forsake this fragrant cot
Which is the home of Enchilat."

*Calling herself
"Enchilat" to
helpeth along
the rhyme scheme.*

"O my blossom!" cried Zapata
(Kicking loose from faithful Lotta),
"Flee with me, my little otter
From this harbor of El Gada."

*Zapata attempteth
to seduce the
lady.*

"On my ship, The S.S. Blotter,"
Swore the passionate Zapata,
"I shall map and I shall plot a
Magic Voyage, Enchilada!"

*He proposeth
a long sea
voyage.*

4

Part III.

Then with scorn did Enchilada,
Catching wind of salty Lotta,
Pinch her nose at Count Zapata
And retire to her cot. "A

*She refuseth,
citing an unpleasant
odor.*

Salty stench!" cried Enchilada.
"Never shall I leave El Gada;
Get thee hence to the Armada!"
Cried the fragrant Enchilada.

*Zapata taketh the
news hard.*

"A pox upon you!" raged Zapata,
"A pox upon your damned Armada!"
Wishing Lotta thus the pox,
Zapata knocked him off the docks.

*He inhospitably
killeth his
companion.*

Afterwards did Count Zapata
Kneel above the sinking Lotta.
"Lotta! Lotta!" moaned Zapata.
"O Cruel Fate! O Enchilada!"

*Should he killeth
himself too? He
keepeth going.*

So it was that Count Zapata
Sailing back to the Armada
Vowed his ship would rot apace
Before he e'er forgot the face,

*He proceedeth to
do penance, and
thus the poem
concludeth.*

The heart, the sight, the words of Lotta
Or that whiff of Enchilada.

Lines Composed Upon an Early Morning Freshman English Class: Dakota University

Dakota has nothing to show more drear:
Downcast of face be he who passes by
This dim-lit cell of White Hall 103!
The Freshmen now do, like pajamas, wear
The stupor of the morning; silent, bare,
Texts, tonsils, intellects and mouths do lie
Open unto the ceiling, and a Sigh
Celestial draws a suction through the air.
Never did Yawn more eloquently speak
Of wint'ry rhetoricians mute and dumb;
Ne'er saw I, never felt a calm so deep—
In my despair ne'er dreamt that it would come
To this—Dear Me! The Freshmen are asleep!
And I—a solitary voice alone!

Epithelmalamion

I.

Sère March! Crisp Mother of Millions! (Her children
    overwhelm her;
For Goddesses and Queens are spawned in March—
    and so was Thelma).
Hear, O March! Shrill month of murdered monarchs,
    month of doom!
(My poems allude to history when there is room.)
O March! O Month! O much-loved month of March,
O beast which enters lion-like and mutton-like departs,
Wild March, but bellow and cruel winter will be gone!
O March, march on, march much, until I end my song.

II.

Fair Helen of Troy was born of March, the folly and the
    fashion!
And so, too, Thelma Wapshingle, the object of my
    passion.
And yet, O March, today we sing of Thelma, not of
    Helen;
For one is dust, the other, ripe and splendid as a melon.
Eternal ripeness shall be hers: she ripens in these lines
While other melons, lacking bards, must wither on their
    vines.
But let them wither! Let them envy Thelma's poem!
O March, march on, march much, until I end my song.

III.

"Ripeness is all!" the player said, and Thelma is all
    ripeness.
A dish of frozen strawberries would be to her a likeness.
—Yet there is nothing cold about her—oh, no! What I
    meant
Was that her ripeness is arrested now, is something
    permanent.
For even you, O March, must fall to April from your
    bough;
But Thelma Wapshingle out-buds the seasons. Saved now
From corrupting Time, she ripens on art's platter;
And though you march and march on much—O March,
    it can't much matter!

Zapata and Enchilada: A Romantic Ballad

Emmett's first successful poetical effort, according to his friend, C. C. Clopp. The idea is based on a story from Boccaccio. It is interesting to note that even in this early poem Emmett is concerned with the theme of sin and repentance (as opposed to Boccaccio, who often liked a good story for its own sake). The rhyme scheme is unusual but not without precedent. Fillipi Manicotti utilized a single rhyme repeated in a series of quatrains in the early sixteenth century, calling his technique *rima schema.* Emmett, however, is the only poet of recent times to use this pattern, which is rather more difficult to execute in English than Italian.

1. *wot:* know. 20. *cot:* cottage.

Lines Composed Upon an Early Morning
Freshman English Class: Dakota University

Here Emmett diverges from the standard rhyme scheme of the Wordsworthian sonnet, varying the usual a-b-b-a, a-b-b-a monotony with a dashing c-d-c-d-c-d finale. No doubt he broke the rules on purpose to achieve a spontaneous effect. The poem gives us an insight to Emmett's experience as a lecturer.

1. *drear:* gloomy. 3. *White Hall 103:* Emmett's classroom.

Epithelmalamion

In this poem Emmett imitates the formal structure of Spenser's "Epithalamion," combining the popular rhythms of the folk ballad with Wagnerian opera. Notice that the basic metrical pattern is iambic polytameter, built on a variation of the eight-foot line, the longest poetical line in many a year. The concluding line of the poem is of particular interest in that it achieves a length of eight feet, three inches, breaking the previous record held by Whitman.

It is worth noting that this is the poem Emmett recited at a picnic the day before Thelma eloped with Obermann. In a very real sense, therefore, *Epithelmalamion* marks the dividing line between Emmett's early songs of innocence and what soon followed.

3. *month of murdered monarchs:* allusion to Julius Caesar, who was murdered on the ides of March. 9. *Helen of Troy:* famous beauty of ancient times; during the Trojan war she entertained the troops.

J. C. B.

BOOK TWO

Emmett and the Duck

Emmett and the Duck

A sudden squawk: the short wings beat alarm
Above the dangling duck. White thighs deployed
By Emmett Byrd, white neck crooked in his arm,
He holds the paddler helpless: Byrd on Bird.

How can these fascinated webbed feet tickle
Emmett's belly through his loosening pants?
And why should any duck in such a pickle
Scorn this god-like offer of romance?

A nipping of the bill diminishes
The length of Emmett's glory; his galoshes
Fall off.

          Being so bedazzled,
And damned sorry, Emmett finishes.
Did anybody spot him in the marshes
Before he let the duck drop, frazzled?

Sonnet 1

Let me not to the marriage of a duck
Admit impediments. Fowl but *seems* foul
That alters what originally was straight
And hastens the remover to remove.
No sooner caught than nipped! O drat the luck!
But by good fortune it was not an owl.
Before, a dream of ducks; behind, a bite.
Mad in pursuit, and in possession howl!
All this the world well knows: the fates do dangle
Blasted hopes in marshy sediment.
What once was rounded now hangs at an angle;
Yet count this not as an impediment.

If this be error proved when beds are tucked,
I never writ, nor ever loved a duck.

Rover Beach
(For Dick and Paula Jesson)

The doggy-doo is thick to-night.
My stomach, too, is full, and Rover seems
To have the trots;—On the Clam Shack the bug bulb
Flickers and is gone; the lakefront, shimmering, stands
Glimmering and swimmering. Litter strews the sand.
Close the windows, foul is the night air!
Cockers, poodles, sheep-dogs and the like despoil the
   land.
Listen! you hear the grating roar
Of people floundering in the muck who find
A dry spot, and returning up the strand,
Begin, and cease, and then again begin
To sink with tremulous cadence slow
Up to their knees in residue.

Sophocles long ago
Put his foot in it by the Agean
And it brought to mind the misery
Of Philoctetes, Oedipus,
The fetid ebb and flow
Of bad luck and the idea of catharsis.

It reminds me
Of my girlfriend, Thelma Wapshingle.
She, too, was at the full and round and soft,
But she deserted me
One moon-blanched night for Izzy Obermann,
The Scholar-Gipsy.

Ah, me! I find eternal sadness in
The breath of the night-wind as it wafts o'er,
For it stirs visions vast and drear
Of starry eyes and mossy haunts
And naked Wapshingles of the world.

Ah, Duck, let us be true
To one another! for the beach which seems
To lie before us like a murky stew,
Putrid, miserable, and full of doggy-doo,
Hath neither joy, nor love, nor light,
Nor music, alcohol, nor colours bright,
Nor funny stories, birds, nor peace of mind,
Nor girls, nor pleasant scenery of any kind.
And we are here on crapulous Rover Beach,
Swept with yowls and confusing fog,
As vicious animals are unleashed
And life goes to the dogs.

The Love Song of Emmett Byrd

Let us go, then, little Duck,
When the marshes are spread out against the muck
Like a hairy turkey basting in the oven.
Let us go, you little sloven,
Through those half-deserted fields
Of recollected orange peels.
Oh, do not make an awful squawk,
Let us take our little walk.

In the gloom the mallards come and go
Talking of Larry, Moe, and Curly Joe.

The yellow chicken cackling in the farmer's yard
(That future bowl of soup) let fall a peep
Then dropped its guard and, half asleep,
Slipped from its perch atop the coop
Into a steaming pile of dung;
And seeing that the pile was deep,
Curled up its feet and died unsung.

And indeed, will there be time
To make a face to meet the soft gaze of a duck
Who flaps her wings and makes a quack
Inquiring if I'm coming back?

Oh, let us go, then, do not dawdle,
Let me watch your little waddle.

And indeed, will there be time
To wonder, "Did I ever? Did I ever?
Poke into that ducky's feathers?"
They will say: "He must be thin!
But how could he have slipped it in?"
Oh, do not ask, "How was it?"
Hold the wings and easy does it.

In the gloom the mallards come and go
Talking of Larry, Moe and Curly Joe.

For I have known them all already, and what's more,
Have paddled out beyond the moors
And clobbered duckies with my oars
Till they were pinned and wriggling on the shore.

Ah, Duck,
I should have kept you at oar's length,
Not knowing your enormous strength!

And was it worth it, after all,
After the quacks, the nipping and the pain
Among the porcelain (for I had lugged a plate
On which I hoped to be your mate);
And was it worth it, after all,
To squeeze the universal out of a ball
And scatter fragments of my scrota
Across that duck pond in Dakota?

No, by God, I am not Zeus,
And would not dare attempt
A swan, a peacock, or a goose.
I thought a duck might do
To swell a dingus, start a scene or two,
Deferential, glad to be of use—but no.

I should have worn a sock
Before exposing myself to the flock.

Oh, Duck, I did it in a hurry;
Passion claimed me in a flurry.
Too long I've lingered in the marsh:
Farewell! I will go home and wash.

Emmett and the Duck

The poems of Book Two shift from an overriding concern with poetic technique toward a growing emphasis on moral content. Here Emmett experiments with life rather than verse, discovering his natural subject matter and developing a broad range of thematic insight. This first poem of the series is remarkable for its dramatic intensity as well as for its obvious prurient interest. The poet achieves a profoundly disturbing effect by narrating the action in the present tense, thereby encouraging the reader to participate through fantasy in the events enacted in the poem. However, the point of view adhered to throughout is Emmett's, not the duck's.

10. galoshes: rubber overshoes. *12. bedazzled:* all mixed up.

Sonnet 1

In this poem Emmett seems to be debating whether to formalize his relationship with his duck in the face of mounting social disapproval. The form of this sonnet certainly owes something to Shakespeare. (I have promised Mr. C. C. Clopp of Charleston, West Virginia to acknowledge that Emmett certainly owes something to him, too—about eighty dollars—but that Mr. Clop considers the debt cancelled.)

2. impediments: things that get in the way. *14. writ:* wrote.

Rover Beach

During the July 4th weekend Emmett brought his common-law duck to Devil's Lake, N.D. on what was to have been their honeymoon. However, the polluted lakefront only added to Emmett's psychological discomfort. The poem, therefore, is a fervent cry for honesty, truth, cleanliness, and loyalty in a world seemingly gone amuck.

Dick and Paula Jesson: local television personalities, Emmett's concept of the ideal couple. *1. doggy-doo:* animal waste. *17. Philoctetes, Oedipus:* charcters in Sophoclean tragedy who had foot problems; Emmett probably identified with them. *39. crapulous:* full of doggy-doo.

The Love Song of Emmett Byrd

By late July Emmett, who was suffering from nervous exhaustion, had decided to break off his affair. (One critic, Seymour Blatz, suggests that part of Emmett's affair already had broken off several weeks earlier, but there is nothing in the poem to support this.) What begins as a love song ends with a stoical attempt at renunciation. This theme would preoccupy Emmett in the coming months. The lyric has a loose, rambling structure united by the poet's process of psychological association.

10. *Larry, Moe, and Curly Joe:* the three graces. *52. dingus:* a small pecker.

BOOK THREE

Strange Fits of Passion

The Second Ducking

Tossing and turning in my narrowing cot,
I cannot tell what's right or not;
Springs fall apart, the bedboards cannot hold;
A Wapshingle is loosed upon the world,
My Thelma girl is loosed, and everywhere
My sheets with salty tears are sluiced.
My poems lack all conviction, while Izzy
Must be full of passionate intensity.

Surely some revelation is at hand:
A revelation! Hardly are those words out
When a vast image from the unconscious
Makes me shout! Somewhere in a murky pond
A shape with a duck's rear and Thelma's face
Is moving its soft thighs. A bond
Is formed: now must I hasten to the sacred place.
And Emmett Byrd, bewildered and alone,
Slouches (as usual) toward the unknown.

Ozzyduckias

I met a duck from a Dakota pond
And saw: two webbed and padded orange feet
Stuck in the mud . . . Above them, beckoning me on,
Half sunk, a bit of heaven lay, whose down,
And wrinkled lip, and tuft as white as snow
Told that its maker well those passions read
Which yet survived, stamped on my fevered brow,
The hand that grabbed the duck, the heart that beat:
Then on the duck's behind these words appeared:
"My name is Ozzy Duck. I am the pet
Of Elmo Duncan, local vet."
This tag I noticed just as I dereared.
A shotgun cracked! Bounding and bare, I fled:
Goodbye to Ozzy Duck and Elmo's lead!

To His Coy Duck

Had we but world enough, and time,
This coyness, duck, would be no crime.
We would sit down and think which way
To waddle or to pass the day.

Thou by Dakota's duck pond strand
Should'st duck weed find: I in the sand
Would love you till the April flood
Arrives to bury us in mud.

But at your back I always hear
Those flapping wings, and hurrying near
From yonder skies, St. Elmo's fire
Peppering me in the mire.

Therefore, while my youthful whoop
Bestirs the waters like duck soup,
Come let us sport us while we may
While Elmo Duncan is away.

Thus, though we cannot make the vet
Stand still, yet we will make him fret.

The Duckhover
(For Ron Wallace)

I caught this morning morning's ducky: dim-
    pled ducky, ducky-wucky, ducky-dooky, dicky
        ducky.
    Of the rolling duck fat underneath I grabbed a hold, and
        (lucky),
"Hi, there, how are you?" cried out. She wrung the water from a
        wimpling wing
In ecstasy! then off, off forth I fell,
    As a plump beaver plopped a log into the pond: the
        hurl and gliding
    Buffeted me off. My heart in hiding
Stirred for a bird,—the feathers tickle, what the hell!

Brute beauty and valor and act, oh, air, pride, plume, "Here,
    Ducky!" AND the fire that breaks from Elmo, then, a
        billion
Buckshot pellets, most dangerous, O my derrière!

    No wonder of it: sheèr lead embèdded in the bòd
Makes pillow down necessity. Ah, me,
    Pot-shot myself: will walk a little odd.

The Second Ducking

Apparently Emmett's attempts at renunciation gave him many a sleepless night. He knew it was wrong to fraternize with ducks, but he could not rid himself of his need for companionship. In the end, he gave in to wild abandon. This poem documents his backsliding. It is also the only poem Emmett began using a dactylic meter (possibly trochaic, depending on how you look at it).

6. *sluiced:* drenched. 7. *Izzy:* Obermann. 17. *Slouches:* Emmett's perennial bad habit aggravated here by his clubfoot, backsliding, and trying to keep up with a dactylic (or trochaic) beat.

Ozzyduckias

Emmett's decision to take up again with ducks led him to a chance encounter with a tagged duck in the game preserve of Elmo Duncan, local veterinarian and back-to-nature food packager. The encounter eventually proved disastrous, as this series of poems indicates. Compare the rhyme scheme of this sonnet with that of *Lines Composed Upon an Early Morning Freshman English Class.* Can you tell the difference? Note the use of *ellipsis* in the third line (little dots) and what Emmett does with his metrical scheme in line eleven just to keep the reader on his toes.

To His Coy Duck

This is one of the few entirely carefree poems Emmett ever wrote. Its philosophy is based on the Roman proverb, *Carpe Duckum,* literally, "Seize the Duck." The lyric's light, bouncing quality is an improvement over the rigid sonnet form, which tends to get tiresome after two or three examples (particularly in Emmett's hands). This poem is partially indebted to the tradition of English metaphysical poetry, as represented by the metaphor in line eleven likening Elmo Duncan to an atmospheric phenomenon.

11. *St. Elmo's fire:* a flamelike appearance sometimes seen in stormy weather at prominent points on a ship; here, buckshot.

The Duckhover

The background events of this poem are confused, yet a picture does emerge. On September 9, 1973 Emmett was admitted to the emergency ward of Holy Sisters of Mercy Hospital in Fulsome suffering from posterior shotgun wounds. The following day he was listed as an outpatient and incarcerated in the county jail on a double charge of sodomy and poaching. The poem dramatizes the events leading up to this reversal.

As a technical accomplishment, *The Duckhover* is clearly one of Emmett's most important breakthroughs. The meter of most English verse is determined by counting syllables and by tapping on the blackboard with a piece of chalk. To convey the rhythm of iambic pentameter, for example, you tap your chalk like this: dă-dá/dă-dá/dă-dá/dă-dá/dă-dá. But in writing *The Duckhover,* Emmett invented a new form of rhythm by holding his breath and hopping around on his bad foot until he collapsed. This new pattern is expressed as follows: clŏmp-clómp/clŏmp-clómp/clŏmp-clómp/clŏmp-clómp/clŏmp/clómp. Inexperienced readers sometimes have difficulty scanning the poem, but if they stopped counting syllables and tried hopping around, the problem would be solved.

Ron Wallace: former instructor of creative writing at Dakota University, an admirer of Emmett's poetry. *5. off, off forth I fell:* a good example of Emmett's new "clomped rhythm." *12. derrière:* backside.

J. C. B.

BOOK FOUR

The Philosophic Mind

To His Duck From Prison

Tell me not (Duck) I am unkind
  When in my prison cell
I pry the shot from my behind,
  Myself from thee, as well.

True, a new mistress have I found,
  Her name (Duck) is Repentance.
And so I shall not come around
  After I serve my sentence.

I'll no more seek thy touch,
  Dear Duck, no matter I adore;
I could not love thee (Duck) so much,
  Loved I not Thelma more.

Ode To a Duck

I.

Hail to thee, blithe Duck!
   Thou never wert no bird,
But in my heart wert thou my Thelma's
   Voice: the sweetest e'er I heard
In profuse strains of unpremeditated pluck.

II.

In the golden tingle
   Of the sunken sun
Dear Thelma Wapshingle
   Ran off with Obermann;
'T was then my love affair with ducks began.

III.

Thou wast not born for death, immortal Duck!
   No mooching scholar gipsy tred thee down;
The voice I hear this night perhaps is heard
   By those who wounded Emmett Byrd:
Perhaps your song will find a path
   To Thelma's heart when, sick of Obermann,
She stands in tears in the Nebraska corn;
   The same that oft-times hath
Charmed the pants off me, and raised a foam
   On perilous Dakota ponds in lands forlorn.

IV.

Duckling, I listen. For many an hour
    I have been half in love with a four-pound bird,
Called you soft names and fed you a few flowers—
    Enough! I thank you for the music I have heard.
Heard quacks are sweet, but quacks unheard
    Are sweeter; therefore, ye soft duck, quack on.

V.

    Though nothing can reverse the luck
Of Thelma in the corn—and Emmett in the duck,
    We will grieve not, rather find
Strength in memory of blithe ducks behind,
    In the soothing thoughts that spring
    Out of fowl and human suffering;
In years that bring the philosophic mind.

VI.

    After many a summer dies the duck
    Downward to darkness on distended wings
    And gathering swallows twitter in the sky
        But no Byrd sings.

Poem On His Twenty-Ninth Birthday

Do not go, lentil, into that cold soup;
Old beans should warm and roast at close of day.
Stave, stave away the coming of the ploop.

Though carrots at the end are known to droop
Because the cook has forked them tenderly, they
Do not go, lentil, into that cold soup.

Potatoes at the end strive to transcend
The malgamating maelstrom of the fray,
They rage, rage, against the coming of the end.

Wild peas we gathered near the chicken coop
All round and green and dying in the day
Do not go shell-shucked into that cold soup.

Onions (foul breath!) more tearful than the yew,
Blind eyes could daze with fumes, for they
Rage, rage against the slopping of the brew.

And you, my lentil, there on the cracked plate,
Curse, bless me now with your fierce tears:
        I poop.
Rage, Bean, against the booming of your fate.
Do not go, lentil, into that cold soup.

To His Duck From Prison

The weeks he spent in prison marked a turning point in Emmett's thinking. *To His Duck From Prison* develops the love versus honor theme prefigured in *Zapata and Enchilada: A Romantic Ballad*. As a sign of penance Emmett served his entire sentence standing up. After he emerged from prison he never touched a duck again. Technically, the poem is unremarkable, a sign, perhaps, of Emmett's new humility.

Ode To a Duck

Critics generally agree that this is Emmett's crowning philosophical achievement, the full flowering of his mature poetic conscience. The poem extends the range of the Romantic ode, tracing the poet's intellectual growth from sodomite to spritual seer. The dramatic situation is as follows. The poet, walking in the woods, hears the distant quacking of a duck and is poked in the eye by a wet branch. In the meditation which follows he identifies the quacking of the duck with his beloved's voice, speculates as to her whereabouts, and then transcends to achieve mystical union with the Unquacked Quacker, the celestial essence of all music. This insight allows the poet to accept life and stop complaining. An autumnal mood suffuses the ode, perhaps because it was written in October.

1. blithe: easy-going. *12. mooching scholar gipsy:* reference to Obermann. *25. quacks unheard:* mental quacks.

Poem On His Twenty-Ninth Birthday

This was Emmett's last completed work. With hindsight, it seems clear that in writing this poem Emmett was moving toward suicide, but who would have thought it possible to move in that direction using such a jolly rhyme scheme? Remarkable, too, is the poem's organic vision. Nearing death, Emmett was acutely conscious of nature's cyclical pattern. Images of vegetation abound, and the entire poem is subjected to the rhythm of the seasons. Some critics regret the writing of this poem and argue that Emmett might have been better off had he stopped with *Ode To a Duck*. This, of course, is a matter of conjecture.

3. ploop: splash. *13. yew:* a gloomy sort of tree. *18. poop:* condition associated with eating too many lentils; also a death image.

J. C. B.

Post Cards

Editor's Introduction

Although he was not a gifted prose writer, Emmett left behind a small body of personal correspondence which, when read in conjunction with his poetry, sheds light on his poetic practice. Reading these jottings can be a profoundly moving human experience, too, for they reveal the stresses, fears, and passions with which Emmett grappled in the final months of his life. The notes addressed to me are particularly valuable, if I may say so, for in these Emmett expresses his theories on aesthetics and freely discusses the progress of his works. In other correspondence with his mother, Thelma, and Obermann, we gain rare glimpses into the homely side of Emmett the young man.

As in his poetry, Emmett's style is terse, personal, and direct. Indeed, he never composed a full letter in his life; the long epistolary form would have been alien to his nature. Instead, Emmett's corpus of outgoing mail consists entirely of picture post cards with only half the blank side open for a writing space, the other half being reserved for the address. Yet already these cards have become a source of great speculation for scholars. Each one bears a reproduction of some great art masterpiece. Winslow Farquhar was able to discover that Emmett collected the cards during his sophomore year while studying for his final exam in art history. Invariably, we believe, Emmett's choice of art work is directly related to the subject matter of the card and perhaps gives us some clue to his hidden feelings at the time of writing. Each card, as it were, contains a surface verbal meaning as well as a hidden symbolic meaning suggested by the art work on the reverse side. Reading Emmett's mail one thus is reminded of Blake, another visionary poet for whom visual and written modes mutually interact to determine meaning.

For the benefit of future scholars I have bracketed the title of the relevant art work under the heading of each post card.

J. C. B.

Post Cards

TO EMMA BYRD

[Michelangelo: *David*]

12 September 1968

Dear Ma,

Please send the jockey shorts I left behind in the bureau in the guest room. School looks o.k. this semester.

Hope you are well.

Love,
Emmett

TO EMMA BYRD

[Botticelli: *The Birth of Venus*]

1 May 1969

Dear Ma,

Guess what? I have developed a passion for my teaching assistant, Thelma Wapshingle. She's a nice girl, and I know you'll like her. Also I've been doing some thinking about my career. Running a drugstore sounds so . . . you know, *bourgeois!* I think I'll be a poet.

Have to run.

Love,
Emmett

[*Editor's note:* Here there occurs a gap in the correspondence of about a year. The bulk of these missing post cards (which number in the dozens) are love notes to Thelma Wapshingle and remain in her possession. Ms. Wapshingle, in conjunction with Professor Isidore Obermann of Nebraska State Teacher's College, has announced her intention of publishing this material sometime next year. —J. C. B.]

TO JOHN CROWE BYRD

[Raphael: *The School at Athens*]

4 April 1970

Dear Uncle Jack,

Thanks for having me over. School is great. I'm sorry Auntie Eleanor got upset at the story I told during supper. I thought she was in the kitchen and couldn't hear. Please apologize for me.

Regards,
Emmett

TO ISIDORE OBERMANN

[Munch: *The Scream*]

13 November 1971

Dear Obermann,

You mean to say you've *lost* my *Enchilada* manuscript? That's half my life's work! Keep looking!

Anxiously,
Emmett

TO ISIDORE OBERMANN
[Bellini: *St. Francis in Ecstasy*]

10 March 1972

Dear Obermann,
    What a relief. I'll pick it up tomorrow.
                                    Yours,
                                    Emmett

TO THELMA WAPSHINGLE
[Rodin: *Cupid and Psyche*]

2 July 1972

Dear Thelma,
    See you Saturday at eight.

                                    XXXXX,
                                    Emmett

TO JOHN CROWE BYRD
[Manet: *Dejeuner sur l'Herbe*]

10 June 1973

Dear Uncle Jack,
    Thelma, Obermann, and I had a picnic out at the
pond this afternoon. It was terrific. We got high and
Thelma took her clothes off while Obermann and I
talked about art. I know you understand all about these
things because you teach poetry. I wish I could tell ma
about it, but you know *her*.
    Obermann recited *Empedocles on Etna* for us and I
recited *Epithelmalamion*. Gee, it was great. Regards to
Auntie Eleanor.

                                    Yours,
                                    Emmett

43

TO EMMA BYRD

[Picasso: *Guernica*]

11 June 1973

Dear Ma,
    Some bad news. Thelma has eloped with Obermann.
Ma, it's so depressing! I'm distraught.

Your
Emmett

TO ISIDORE OBERMANN

[Poussin: *The Rape of the Sabine Women*]

12 June 1973

Dear Obermann,
    First my *Enchilada* manuscript, now this. You turd.

Emmett

TO THELMA WAPSHINGLE

[Pollaiuolo: *Martyrdom of St. Sebastian*]

13 June 1973

Dear Thelma,
    No hard feelings.

Good luck,
Emmett

TO JOHN CROWE BYRD

[Van Gogh: *Self-Portrait with Bandaged Ear*]

27 June 1973

Dear Uncle Jack,

I must tell you what a terrible state I've been in in the weeks since Thelma left me. I have been living by myself out in the woods trying to commune with nature. I find that I can relate very well to ducks even though I'm distraught. There's quite a bit to be learned from ducks. Some are more loyal than people. The trouble is, they nip. I'm writing a poem about this called *Emmett and the Duck,* which I will send tomorrow. Regards to Auntie Eleanor.

Yours,
Emmett

TO JOHN CROWE BYRD

[Caravaggio: *Young Bacchus*]

16 July 1973

Dear Uncle Jack,

Thank you for the high praise for *Emmett and the Duck.* I feel I have hit my stride as a poet and that I have much work to do despite my constant pain and suffering. I have written several new poems about ducks and am conducting research in the field. Tell Auntie Eleanor not to worry.

Regards,
Emmett

[Rembrandt: *The Anatomy Lesson of Dr. Tulp*]

25 September 1973

Dear Ma,

Sorry I haven't been home in the last two weeks to answer the phone, but I was detained elsewhere. I also had to undergo some minor surgery for removal of buckshot. It was the result of a small hunting accident and a case of mistaken identity, so don't you believe anything else you might hear. Anyhow, I'm a reformed man.

As for my birthday, I really don't want any presents, just a card.

With love,
Emmett

TO EMMA BYRD
[Grünewald: *Crucifixion*]

31 October 1973

Dear Ma,

Am down in the dumps again today. Nothing to worry about.

Thanks for the card.

Farewell,
Your loving son

Backgrounds to Criticism

From *The Fulsome Messenger,* October 31, 1973:

EMMETT BYRD DEAD AT 29
Poet Plunges To His Death
Was the Subject of a Dissertation

Fulsome, N.D. (AP)—Emmett Byrd, the noted poet, plunged to his death today when he fell from a stepladder while trying to change a bulb in his downtown apartment. Friends said that Byrd had been despondent in recent weeks since the disappearance of his fiancee, Thelma Wapshingle, a graduate student at Dakota University, where Byrd was an instructor. Authorities declined to speculate whether the poet's death would be ruled an accident or suicide. An autopsy is expected.

Though no note was found on the body, a poem was pinned to Byrd's outside shirt pocket, according to Arvin Shimkis, County Coroner. "If you ask me, that poem really isn't any good," said Shimkis, who spoke to reporters early this morning. "Of course," he added, "I'm no literary critic. I suppose we'll have to wait and see whether it will stand the test of time."

The poem, entitled *Poem On His Twenty-Ninth Birthday,* suggests that Byrd may have been depressed about growing old.

"This is terrible!" said Winslow Farquhar, a local Ph.D. candidate who had been writing a dissertation on Byrd's poems. Contacted by a reporter, Farquhar stated, "Emmett was a very sensitive person." In response to further questioning, he added: "It will be difficult to complete my dissertation now that Emmett Byrd is gone, but I owe it to his memory to continue."

According to Farquhar, Byrd was writing furiously in the months preceding his death, and many of his poems remain to be published. "It's a fantastic research opportunity," he added, "but a great voice has been forever stilled."

Emmett Byrd came to Dakota in 1966. Residents of the campus area will remember the poet for his eccentric manner of dress and brushes with the law. It is not known if Byrd is survived by any relatives. Funeral arrangements have not yet been announced.

DISSERTATION APPROVAL FORM
DEPARTMENT OF ENGLISH
Dakota University

NAME: _____Winslow Farquhar_____

THESIS DIRECTOR: _John Crowe Byrd, Ph.D._

PROPOSED TITLE OF DISSERTATION:

Downward to Darkness on Distended Wings:

The Early Poetry of Emmett Byrd

1. *Summarize the present state of research on this subject and the need for further work.*

Emmett Byrd is perhaps the most signifi-
cant new poet on the horizon, but as yet
little has been written on his work
(partly because little of his work has
yet appeared). However, the forthcoming
publication of his collected poems, <u>Byrd
Thou Never Wert</u>, will, according to
Seymour Blatz, "assure Byrd's rank among
the one or two very best poets of his
generation, irrespective of age." Another
dissertation on Emmett Byrd was begun two

51

years ago by Maggie Dribble, a graduate
student in linguistics, but due to the
fire which destroyed Crowe Hall last winter
(where she took meals and kept her notes),
it is doubtful that her work will be completed (even if she responds to therapy).

2. *State what you propose to do.*

Since no full length critical study has
yet been published on Byrd's poetry, this
thesis will serve as a comprehensive and
general introduction. Because Mr. Byrd
currently is working on his later verse
(he is still young), the focus of this
thesis will deal chiefly with his early
poems and post cards. I propose to study
the influence of Wordsworth and Coleridge
on several of these early poems, particularly the matter of Byrd's debt to
nineteenth century sonnet and ballad forms
in such works as Lines Composed Upon an
Early Morning Freshman English Class and
Zapata and Enchilada: A Romantic Ballad.
I will also delve into phenomenology and

epistemology in discussing his most
puzzling work, <u>Thirteen Ways of Looking
at a Crowe Byrd</u>. (This poems unfortu-
nately, has been lost--M.C.H.) And I will
talk about a lot of things in between.
My main idea is to prepare the groundwork
for a subsequent study on the development
of Byrd's later poetry (the growth of the
poet's mind, and so on) as soon as the
later poetry gets written. There is a
strong possibility of my getting an
interview with Emmett Byrd which might
be incorporated into the thesis.

Approved by Thesis Director

John Crowe Byrd

Date _10/15/73_

The Poet Speaks

Note: The following interview with Emmett Byrd was conducted on October 28, 1973 by Winslow Farquhar. Had Emmett lived, the interview would have been expanded. Had Farquhar lived, it would have been included in his dissertation.

J. C. B.

FARQUHAR: What is it that makes you want to write poetry, Mr. Byrd?

EMMETT: Pain. I am a very sensitive person.

FARQUHAR: Do you mean mental anguish or physical pain?

EMMETT: Both. Life for me is a vale of tears.

FARQUHAR: Would you say, then, that your basic philosophy of life is pessimistic?

EMMETT: I wouldn't say that.

FARQUHAR: What things in life, then, give you happiness?

EMMETT: Nature. Ducks.

FARQUHAR: Speaking of ducks, is it true, as some critics have remarked, that your poetry is heavily autobiographical?

EMMETT: The way I look at it, I write for the ages.

FARQUHAR: But wouldn't you also say that you have been influenced by the contemporary trend of very personal, confessional verse?

EMMETT: Confessional verse?

FARQUHAR: By confessional verse I mean a kind of poetry that combines a traditional concern for broad universal themes with the lyrical expression of personal emotion drawing on the immediate experience of the poet.

EMMETT: So?

FARQUHAR: Don't you write that kind of poetry?

EMMETT: No.

FARQUHAR: Then I take it that you feel reluctant to discuss details of your personal life in this interview?

EMMETT: Reluctant is the word.

FARQUHAR: Well, which poets writing today do you admire the most?

EMMETT: T. S. Eliot.

FARQUHAR: But T. S. Eliot is dead.

EMMETT: He is? What a blow.

FARQUHAR: Do you have any other poets you admire?

EMMETT: Don't tell me they're *all* dead.

FARQUHAR: Well, who?

EMMETT: Yeats?

FARQUHAR: Dead.

EMMETT: Pound?

FARQUHAR: Dead.

EMMETT: E. A. Robinson? Edgar Lee Masters? Siegfried Sassoon?

FARQUHAR: I'm sorry, but—

EMMETT: Conrad Aiken?

FARQUHAR: Just died a few weeks ago.

EMMETT: I'm depressed.

FARQUHAR: I'm sorry if I've upset you. Would you care to talk about some other aspect of your poetry?

EMMETT: No.

FARQUHAR: Perhaps we could continue this interview a little later.

EMMETT: I'm just not in the mood right now.

FARQUHAR: Well, I want to thank you for agreeing to be interviewed in the first place.

EMMETT: Don't mention it.

FARQUHAR: You know, one of the things I particularly wanted to ask you about was your attitude toward rhyme. Maybe we could talk about that another time.

EMMETT: What about it?

FARQUHAR: I was wondering, do you feel, as Robert Frost once said, that writing poetry without rhyme is like playing tennis without a net?

EMMETT: Did Frost say that?

FARQUHAR: Yes.

EMMETT: Is *he* dead, too?

FARQUHAR: I'm afraid so.

EMMETT: Gosh.

FARQUHAR: Forgive me, I'm leaving. But can we continue later on, perhaps?

EMMETT: Okay, okay.

FARQUHAR: Goodbye, Mr. Byrd, and thank you.

EMMETT: Goodbye. I'm so depressed.

Select Bibliography

(compiled by J. C. B.)

CRITICISM

Blatz, Seymour, "Pope's Influence on Emmett Byrd," *Publications of the Modern Language Association of America* (November, 1973), 101-120.

Byrd, John Crowe, "Pope's Lack of Influence on Emmett Byrd: A Reply to Seymour Blatz," *Ball State University Forum* (December, 1973), 62-74.

Byrd, John Crowe, "Byrd's Knowledge of Ornithology," *Frankfurter Arbeiten aus dem Gebiete der Anglistik und der Amerika-Studien* (January, 1974), 4-5.

Byrd, John Crowe, "Some Bird Imagery in *Ode To a Duck*," *Dakota Quarterly* (February, 1974), 8-26.

Farquhar, Winslow, "The Relation of Art and Biography in Emmett's Post Cards," Chapter I of an unfinished Ph.D. dissertation (Dakota University, 1973).

Ferret-Pickforth, Roland, "Brute Beauty: Versification and Contortions in *The Duckhover*," *Transactions of the Cambridge Bibliographical Society* (November, 1974), 346-362.

Mauve, Hugh Selwyn, "A Nipping of the Bill: Pain and Transfiguration in the Poems of Emmett Byrd," *West Virginia University Philological Papers* (Winter, 1974), 12-21.

Neuilly-Prat, François, "Byrd's Debt to Yeats: A Possible Source for *Emmett and the Duck*," *Mémoires de la Société Néophilologique de Helsinki* (Spring, 1974), 14-16.

61

Obermann, Isidore, "The *Enchilada* Manuscript: A Textual Analysis," *The Journal of Opposite Citation* (April, 1974) 44-108.

Pellagra, Gilbert, "To Waddle or to Pass the Day: Emmett Byrd's Poetry of Paradox," *Journal of the Australasian Universities Language and Literature Association* (May 1974), 186-207.

Quasimodo, Hippolyte, "The Love Versus Honor Theme in *To His Duck From Prison*," *Benedictine Review* (August, 1974), 8-23.

Secaucus, Milo, "Perilous Dakota Ponds: Emmett Byrd as Naturalist," *Boy's Life* (Summer, 1974), 12-17.

Trask, H. K., "Ducking the Issue: Sexism in the Poems of Emmett Byrd," *Ms. Magazine* (September, 1974), 1-9.

Von Weltschmerz, Wilhelm, *"Zapata and Enchilada:* A Linguistic Model," *The Semi-Quarterly Review of Semiotics* (December, 1974), 15-31.

Winnington-Wattle, J. P., "Myth, Ritual, and Vegetables in *Poem On His Twenty-Ninth Birthday:* A Structuralist Approach," *The Journal of Imminent Discovery* (February, 1975), 8-47.

BIOGRAPHY

Clopp, Isabella, "I Remember Emmett," *Reader's Digest* (May, 1971), 126-132.

Eddle, Leon, *After Many a Summer Dies the Duck: A Biography of Emmett Byrd.* 3 Volumes. Oxford. 1974.

Sauerbraten, Howard T. *Byrd and His Circle: Influence, Literary Relations, and Just Plain Relations.* Chicago. 1975.

Obermann, Isidore and Thelma Wapshingle, ed. *Emmett in Love: Cards, Notes, and Recollected Telephone Conversations of Emmett Byrd, 1969-1973.* (Forthcoming from Nebraska State Teacher's College Press.)

Litmus, Oleander. *Emmett Byrd: The Marvelous Summer.* (Forthcoming from Alfred K. Knopf.)

Schpilkawitz, Mark. *Freely and Without Shame: The Love Ethic of Emmett Byrd.* (Forthcoming from Twayne's World Author Series.)

Wapshingle, Thelma, as told to Isidore Obermann. *The Object of His Passion: Memoirs of a Teaching Assistant.* (Forthcoming from Dakota University Press.)

Index of Titles and First Lines

(W.F.)